Awesome—this is so refreshing!

Cindy Noonan, author, *Dark Enough to See the Stars: A Story of Escape on the Underground Railroad*

I always enjoy how Sherry takes truth and shares it with an artsy, new-to-me twist, causing me to look at life in a different—and BIGGER way!

Sarah Lynn Phillips, freelance writer; blogger, *Penned Without Ink: Trusting God to Write Your Story*

Enjoy But-Kickers on YouTube
(https://www.youtube.com/c/SherryBoykinBut-Kickers)
More Information
https://www.But-Kickers.com

But-Kickers
Growing Your Faith Bigger Than Your "But!"

Thirty Powerful Must-Reads for Growing Faith and Kicking "Buts"

For President and Mrs. Carter,

Sherry Boykin

But-Kickers Books
Clarks Summit, Pennsylvania

Thank you for serving our country and for nourishing our souls!

Sherry D Boykin
5-20-2021

Published by But-Kickers Books
a division of
But-Kickers: Growing Your Faith Bigger Than Your "But!"
538 Venard Rd.
Clarks Summit, PA 18411
www.but-kickers.com

Printed in the United States of America

ISBN-13: 978-0692387764

ISBN-10: 0692387765

Contents

To my God, my B, and my Kaki, who bless me by kicking my "buts" every single day.

Growing Your Faith Bigger Than Your "But"

Tired of squeezing a size twelve "but" into a size five faith? Consider these three keys to overcoming mediocrity:

Exercise Your Faith for Something More than Your Salvation

Dare to let your faith count for something more than saving you from frying to a crisp in eternity. Think about that friend who needs to see God as the forgiver of abortions, affairs, or deceit. Or consider that neighbor who needs to know there's a road back from theft, child abandonment, or drug addiction.

And what about that emotional widow whose husband still lives, that postpartum mom who cannot connect with her baby, or that molested teen who feels like filthy trash? Don't they need to hear the hope and feel the hug of God for them specifically—something beyond, "Believe on the Lord Jesus Christ and you will be saved"? Something that doesn't require the leaving of this life in order to find a tidbit of respite?

Let your faith story speak for itself, and let it speak in the raw—as it really happened, not as you hoped it would. Did your husband cheat on you and then wrap it all up with "Sorry"? How did you ever get up out of bed the day after you found out? Be the one person who tells the next sister, who lives through that same horror, how God showed you it wasn’t your fault. Tell how He soothed your rage and how long it took you to stop breaking things every time you thought about betrayal.

Don't treat your faith story like a boyfriend with a police record; it shouldn’t be a secret.

Tell her you get it.

Do you have a history of pretending your way through Christianity while struggling to find emotional stability?

Do you wonder why it took years for someone—for anyone, to tell you it was possible to take anti-depressants and follow Christ at the same time?

Don't treat your faith story like a boyfriend with a police record; it shouldn’t be a secret.

Help someone else discover what radical life and radical change look like from the inside out.

Risk Something

Risk your sense of logic, your misplaced security in your circumstances or surroundings, your reputation. And don't just risk these things—replace them with that illogical, fearful, threatening, or potentially embarrassing thing you would never, EVER do were it not for the specific leading of the Lord to do something by faith.

If you need God to do what is logical or predictable, to travel on the road well-paved, to look good or pious among your peers, to see your 2.3 kids excel, or to just do what you've always done and not take the risk, then you need to put this down and read *Faithless Me* instead.

Risking something means you might just find yourself apologizing to your kids, giving until it literally hurts, taking rebuke from that girl you mentored ten years ago, selling your house and moving to where no one looks like you, disclosing your social or sexual history to judgmental people, or sending your kids to public school—who knows? Just let it be for the ultimate glory of God, not for protecting your own hide.

Risk being wrong about something. Sometimes it is in our wrongness, and our willingness to admit it, that we see miracles happen in the lives of other people.

Toot God's Horn Instead of Jumping on Bandwagons

Join the post-pubescent world, and read the Bible for yourself.

Will you find some confusing things in there?

Sure.

But you're not likely to emerge from the experience confused over the crystal clear admonitions to love your neighbor as yourself, to love your enemies, or to pray for those who despitefully use you.

You *are* likely to emerge from the experience convinced that faith has everything to do with what you would never do as opposed to what Jesus would never do.

Jumping on bandwagons often means throwing someone else under the caravan in order to make yourself look better. Shameful.

Remember Dr. Seuss' children's story about fictional animals called *The Sneetches*? Beach-dwelling, star-bellied Sneetches think they are better than beach-dwelling, bare-bellied Sneetches. The star-bellies, therefore, belittle and exclude the others from their activities and teach their children to do the same.

Then one day a stranger arrives with a machine that adds stars to bellies. The bare-bellies are thrilled for a chance to be part of the "in" crowd, and pretty soon all the Sneetches look alike. This, of course, enrages the original star-bellies because they are no longer an exclusive club.

Eventually, the original star-bellies find the other Sneetches are great fun to have around, the originals abandon their efforts towards exclusivity, and they all live happily ever after.

You can identify the representative protagonists in this story and connect the dots yourself.

Kids get this story right away.

We should, too.

So, the next time your default response to the call for big faith is, BUT I can't, because . . . , remember that you serve a Lord who loves nothing more than to do the otherwise impossible and to make the whole world say, "Wow, that has to be a God thing!"

Now to him who is able to do immeasurably more than all we ask or imagine, according to his power that is at work within us . . .
~ Ephesians 3:20

"Why Would God Say Something Like *THAT?*"

My feisty little seven-year-old was fit to be tied. We had just finished reading a Bible story, and she was overwhelmed with what seemed to her an outrageous, unfair, one-sided, mean thing to say on the part of God.

What Abraham *Can* Believe

She had heard the story of Abraham, the Hebrew big shot and proverbial friend of God, who tells a lie so big I wonder if his nose might have grown a bit. The faith-filled patriarch can believe God to guide him from his comfortable home in metropolitan Ur to some undisclosed, mystery land while he wanders around tent-dwelling and cow chip-jumping with his post-menopausal wife who will somehow bear his offspring.

What Abraham *Can't* Believe
But Abraham can't believe God will spare his life once foreign men see the beauty of Sarah, his wife, since they will undoubtedly want to take her for their own.

May we all have husbands so bedazzled by our perfect facial symmetry.

So when Abraham travels to a foreign land, he tells the king that Sarah is his sister.

And he tells Sarah to say that he is her brother.

And she does.

The Hiccup
Never mind that weird little thing about them actually being half-siblings that evokes all kinds of icky discomfort—that will have to be fodder for another day's fire. Let's just understand that Abraham lies to save his own rear end, and Sarah goes along with it.

The Plot Thickens
The king is delighted to hear Sarah is Abraham's sister, and so at the suggestion of his men, he takes her to be his own wife. Now listen to how the rest of the story unfolds in the soap opera of Genesis 20:

> [2-3] So Abimelech, king of Gerar, sent for Sarah and took her. But God came to Abimelech in a dream that night and told him, "You're as good as dead—that

woman you took, she's a married woman."

4-5 Now Abimelech had not yet slept with her, hadn't so much as touched her. He said, "Master, would you kill an innocent man? Didn't he tell me, 'She's my sister'? And didn't she herself say, 'He's my brother'? I had no idea I was doing anything wrong when I did this."

6-7 God said to him in the dream, "Yes, I know your intentions were pure, that's why I kept you from sinning against me; I was the one who kept you from going to bed with her. So now give the man's wife back to him. He's a prophet and will pray for you—pray for your life. If you don't give her back, know that it's certain death both for you and everyone in your family."

17-18 Then Abraham prayed to God and God healed Abimelech, his wife and his maidservants, and they started having babies again. For God had shut down every womb in Abimelech's household on account of Sarah, Abraham's wife. (Genesis 20:2-7; 17-18, *The Message*)

Huh?

So the guy who knows God tells a big old fat one and gets the guy who doesn't know God in trouble.

But it's the guy who doesn't know God who is punished while the devout liar walks away unscathed.

I felt my seven-year-old's frustration the first time I heard that story, and a whole lot of other stories just like it.

Seemed like God would have a better handle on His people.

Or like His people would have a better handle on God.

Or like life would work out more agreeably for people who do right things than it would for people who do wrong things.

The But-Kicker

Then it occurred to me that those kinds of stories are fairy tales, and that the Bible does not fall under that umbrella. God's Word is not primarily the story of great pillars of the faith deserving of God's praise and our imitation. It is the story of God's grace and redemption in the life of the proud, short-sighted, unfaithful, lying, adulterous screw-ups who can't find their way to the only porch with a light on—even with a heavenly GPS to show the way.

The pitifully imperfect.

Just like you and me.

So, do God's stories *ever* turn out how we wish they would?

Sure.

But whether they do or not, process, timing, and purpose are key to what God does and to how He does it.

Jesus, for instance, *is* miraculously and gloriously resurrected from His tomb to live forevermore.

But He is betrayed, abandoned, and slain to get there.

The good of Jesus is that He not only overcomes death but that He also overcomes life.

At any point between betrayed and slain a casual onlooker might have said nothing Jesus was doing was worth it, that what he endured—the process, was ridiculous and unfair.

And if not for Christ's overall purpose of redemption, that casual onlooker would be right.

The good of Jesus is that He not only overcomes death but that He also overcomes life.

So the next time you wonder, *Why would God say something like That?* or the next time all you can say in response to God's work is, "Huh?" be glad. Let it serve as proof that the working of His process, timing, and purpose are in place.

And let it serve also as evidence of how completely different He is from how we expect Him to be and how He often does what we least expect Him to do.

"For my thoughts are not your thoughts, neither are your ways my ways," declares the LORD.
~ Isaiah 55:8

Bread and Butter: The New Premarital Sex

Is it me, or does it seem that lately any consumption of food that isn't organic, raw, vegan, or gluten and GMO-free has usurped the position of premarital sex as the prime offender in the Christian church?

Seriously, just go up to four or five church ladies this week and mention something about meat and potatoes, white rice, or juice you didn't boil yourself and sift through cheesecloth. Then count the number of them who squirm in their seats, drop their gaze to the floor, or grab your hand as they lament your descent from God's favor.

And heaven help you if you admit giving this food to your kids.

You'll have no recourse once you let "hot dog" or "funnel cake" slip out of your mouth while you describe your day at the amusement park with your children.

Sympathy

Don't get me wrong. I don't like pink slime, pesticide-drenched blackberries, or corn that has the same DNA as paper plates. And as one who recovered from an Amazon jungle-borne parasite infection with the help of a naturopath and a mostly raw food diet, I am extremely sympathetic to the good-food cause.

I just don't like its growing reputation as the barometer used to determine spirituality. No one is going to hell because they bought the blue-light special for $1.99 per pound and cooked it up for dinner.

A True Story

It used to be that health food geeks were the ones most likely to blow someone away for their adherence to a diet on which the geeks' own mothers probably raised *them*.

When doctors thought I had multiple sclerosis, I went to a health food store in search of something that might alleviate the more uncomfortable symptoms I experienced. I asked one of their gurus for help. Here's what she said:

> Maybe other people's lives are a bit too full with real life to share the church ladies' increasing obsession with fermented things and produce grown in Lancaster County by guys named Jedidiah.

"By the way, do you have bread and butter in your house?"

"Sure," I responded.

"Well, of COURSE you have M.S.!"

I guess she set ME straight! I put everything down and left.

Church Ladies

Now church ladies are doing that same thing. Sadly, there's a real failure to understand where real people are in real life. A while ago I asked a church lady if I could get her some water. She took out her BPA-free water bottle and said, "No, thank you," explaining that *her* water had more oxygen than *my* water.

Maybe other people's lives are a bit too full with real life to share the church ladies' increasing obsession with fermented things and produce grown in Lancaster County by guys named Jedidiah.

Maybe they can't justify $8.99 for a single organic chicken breast in an already stretched budget.

Maybe they believe God will provide everything they need and that God will bless to their bodies everything for which they give thanks.

Maybe they believe moderation of food is a more important issue than fertilization of food.

So—go ahead. Be passionate. Share the wealth of information you have that can help people.

But please, PLEASE stop acting as though the Holy Spirit cannot indwell a temple containing processed food or as though a French fry stuck in a vanilla scoop is a sign of the indulger's slip-slide toward fire and brimstone.

And do have that hummus and asparagus for lunch, but every once in a while, spread it on a piece of rye—just for humanity's sake.

. . . Jesus answered, "I am the way, the truth, and the life. No one comes to the Father except through me . . ."
~ John 14:6

How to Get Your Millennial to Take Your Advice

Crazy, right? You carry them, scream them out, wipe their butts, and snuggle with them through nightmares and thunderstorms. Then the day comes when they need life-defining advice, and they run from you as fast as they can and find someone else to help them connect the dots.

Ever wonder why?

I have.

Even though my only child is still too busy making leprechaun traps and planning snuggle parties to engage in life-defining conversations longer than thirty seconds, dorm-parenting for fifteen years on a college campus has given me loads of insight as to why your Millennial struggles to take your advice. It's not that you don't mean well, and they know that. But if you're parenting teens or young adults, your fundamental way of thinking is so different from theirs that they often get tired of trying to jump the gap. They literally cannot get to the planet on which you live, and so they opt for someone local.

The good news in this is that any attempt you make to reverse the thinking patterns, I've listed below, will produce a response from your Millennial that makes you high-five your reflection as you see a renewed desire in them to hear what you have to say. Here's what I mean:

You're Offended By the Question, "Why?"
The very idea of "Why?" implies that just because you said it is not enough—regardless of what *it* is. That you are an authority figure in the life of your Millennial doesn't carry the weight you think it should. They constantly ask you to back up what you say with some sort of proof.

To you, it's a little like asking who else will be at the party before deciding if you'll invest your time in going. If your default answer to "Why?" has ever been, "Because I said so," or worse yet, "Because I said so, and I'm bigger than you," you know exactly what I mean.

Your Millennial sees "Why?" as a means to further understanding and assurance; you see it as an insult. After all, *you* just accepted what your authorities said, right?

Answer that “Why?” question and do so sincerely.

Just watch what happens.

You're Reluctant to Admit There's More than One Way to Skin a Cat

I really get this one. I practically live in it. That whole "your truth/my truth" thing Millennials wear on their shirt sleeves can be maddening, can't it? And that's especially true for anyone who insists on calling a spade a spade.

But I have to tell you: if you're keeping score, the Millennials win on this one, hands down. Even God doesn't treat every situation, called by the same name, in the same, exact way.

Face it.

Abraham lied, and someone else got in trouble (Genesis 20). Ananias and Sapphira lied, and they dropped dead (Acts 5).

Apparently there's more to this than meets the eye. Your Millennial loves to get to the heart of issues, but their parents often want a safe, easy answer. After all, there's nothing to discuss if someone is guilty of lying, is there?

It will take the honest disclosure of something you’re not proud of, but if you are brave enough to share your sin, something for which you would have been “toast” if not for God’s direct intervention, your Millennial will see that you understand grace as much as you understand truth, and that they can trust you when it’s their turn to disclose sin.

You Are Completely Sold Out to Stuff You Hate

This one probably scares your Millennial the most. It could be your job (you call it having a good work ethic—they call it death of a dream), your propensity to say yes to things because you "can't" say no (you call it the gift of service—they call it bondage), or your willingness to commit to what is accepted by your culture even if it defies following your own heart (you call it godliness—they call it a lie).

Agree with your daughter or son that ceasing to pray about and pursue your dream altogether is, at least on some level, a betrayal of who God made you to be.

Frankly, your Millennial would rather die than be described this way. And if taking your advice on those life-defining decisions puts them even an inch closer to being like this, they are too busy shaking in their boots to even consider it.

Agree with your daughter or son that ceasing to pray about and pursue your dream altogether is, at least on some level, a betrayal of who God made you to be.

Tough words? Go ahead and review the real-life dilemma of having to pay bills and support kids, but I bet they can finish any sentence you begin with that argument. And believe it or not, they know this is a true and viable excuse. But something deep inside them (dare I call it the Spirit?) tells them there are possibilities for their lives that will never come to fruition if they don't believe a great, big God for great, big things.

Attempt to see it their way. Open that discussion.

One great way to resist discouragement with issues like this is to remember that God is so universal that He appeals to the one who doubts absolute truth as easily as He appeals to the one who needs a straight path and blinders or to the one who needs to smell smoke before he realizes he's on fire.

Now you've heard it. What will you do?

To the Jews I became like a Jew, to win the Jews . . . To the weak I became weak, to win the weak. I have become all things to all people so that by all possible means I might save some. I do all this for the sake of the gospel that I may share in its blessings.
~ I Corinthians 9:20-23

Profile Me, Please!

Gone are the days when I lamented hyphenated first name intros like, "This is Sherry—the girl who's still single," or "Remember Sherry—that jungle missionary I told you about?"

Still Single . . .

It wasn't the fact of being "still single" or being a missionary that troubled me. The presumptuous profiling that went along with it is what made me roll my eyes. People's assumption that I was on my way to being a bun-wearing recluse with a house full of cats pushed them to set me up with some of the sorriest relationship prospects north and south of the border. That includes two spies, one who got me to go out with him by pretending to be on a date with another woman.

Long story.

. . . And a Missionary, too

And that missionary thing brought forth every guy wanting to practice-preach or try out his best gringo Spanish on a sitting-duck date. They assumed my *missionary-ness* meant I wanted a guy who knew nothing more or spoke of nothing else besides church and cherubs.

One of those dates was so unbearable that when the guy drove me home that night in Frostbite, Indiana, and I realized I had forgotten my keys AND that none of my roommates were home, I hid in the vestibule until I was sure my date had driven away. I just couldn't listen to him parse Greek verbs any longer.

The BUT-Kicker

But the BUT-Kicker about all this is that the initial profiling is what made the unfolding of God's story through my life seem much more noteworthy. That I'm no longer single is not the God-moment I'm talking about. The God-prints here are that I never presented myself as that bun-wearing, cat-loving recluse, that I didn't settle for a guy who needed permission from a parole officer to take me out on a date, and that I avoided capture by the man too insecure to read the Bible on his phone since no one would hear him turn its pages.

All of this points to God. Despite how everyone profiled me, those things never became my reality.

It's reminiscent of Rahab—always identified as a harlot, and, in fact, as *the* harlot (Joshua 2). But when she shows up in the genealogy of Christ (Matthew 1), her former profile as harlot is swallowed up in glory.

When Elisabeth, "who was said to be unable to conceive" (Luke 1:36), gives birth to John the Baptist, again, all attention points to God.

And when He, who knew no sin—He, who was called "Mighty God . . . Prince of Peace" (Isaiah 9:6) becomes sin for us, the veil in the temple is torn, darkness covers the land in the middle of the day, and our salvation is purchased.

So, go ahead—let them profile you! Then savor the unveiling of God's unpredictable story in your life!

I am God, and there is no other; I am God, and there is none like me . . . What I have said, that I will bring about; what I have planned, that I will do.
~ Isaiah 46:9-11

A Call to Biblical Manhood: Whose Job Is It to Keep His Pants Up?

SOMEONE, help me with this—please! Just how responsible are women for maintaining the sexual purity of men? If you've ever been part of an institution that requires its girls or women to present themselves as if they've shopped at the mercantile and spruced up at the apothecary, you know what I mean.

Is it true that men have no control over their bodies once their eyes are engaged in the art of seeing?

Insecurity

I do not condone padded push-ups/push-outs, tight, navel-touching deep V's, or short, sheer bottoms that reveal the brand or cut of undergarments a woman is wearing. I actually feel sorry for anyone who resolves all her insecurity issues at the checkout counter in the Skank department.

But I also feel sorry for those who refuse to call a lace-bibbed, bow-tied dress on a forty-year-old the abomination that it is. These are two extremes of an issue on which the Christian world cannot get a grip.

A Common Misconception

The idea that men are greater spiritual giants when surrounded by women in gunny sacks is a misconception that moves our attention from the real issue—immature men—and borders on misogyny.

What about Real Life?

This misconception leads to the development of men who can't function in a secular work environment, at the mall, or at the beach where, perchance, they encounter women dressed like regular people. Sinful perhaps, but regular, just the same. If the man in this scenario falls into sin, is it the fault of the regular women he encounters, or is something else at play here?

It also leads to the development of godly woman wannabes who insist on wearing the same Laura Ingalls-inspired fashion their prepubescent daughters are wearing. Since when is *godly* a synonym for *juvenile?*

A True Story
Not long ago, I was asked to attend a weeks-long seminar for college students. After a few sessions, one of the seminar leaders asked if I would talk to a girl who always sat in the front row of the horseshoe-designed seating arrangement. Other girls would normally fill in where this early bird was already seated, and the leaders would usually sit in the center section of the horseshoe.

The guys, who typically arrived later than everyone else, would sit directly across from the girl I was asked to approach. The seminar leader said a few of the guys were distracted by this very attractive girl who always wore a dress and who always crossed her legs. He wanted me to ask her to sit elsewhere, uncross her legs, or develop a more muted sense of fashion.

It took at least a week for me, an outspoken, middle-aged woman who had worked more than a decade with college students, to even think about approaching this girl. Why? Because she was so appropriately dressed and poised that I actually felt stupid.

It's not like I'd be approaching her about any wrong she had done, I reasoned. *This would be a call to help her brothers in Christ—to help them concentrate on what was being presented, and nothing else.* I still felt like something was wrong with that whole picture, but I didn't know what.

Another week passed.

Then came the BUT-Kicker. Right around week five, I walked into the seminar and realized someone had forgotten to set up the chairs in the usual design. And when the guys arrived, there were ample seats available far *behind* the pretty girl—ample seats that were a God-send for frustrated men whose eyes might otherwise be caught up in the art of seeing what they said was so distracting, what they claimed they could not handle.

Where do you think they sat?

On Pavlov and Dogs

Yep. Like Pavlovian dogs, they sat directly across from the pretty girl who always wore a dress and who always crossed her legs. I respectfully declined the request to approach the girl and offered to approach the guys instead.

Where are the men who will stop acting like victims of Victoria's Secret, and who will make a choice for what is obvious, good, and right?

Where are the older men who can tell young guys what to do with dangerous thoughts that could end up on their "regret" list for years to come?

Is it fair to even imply that God's goodness and power are in play only in the absence of enticing things?

Where are the blood-washed, sanctified warriors who will fight for fidelity and stop blaming women for exciting passions that could just as easily be channeled into God's glory as into the gutter?

When I was a child, I spoke like a child, I thought like a child, I reasoned like a child. When I became a man, I gave up childish ways.
~ I Corinthians 13:11

Why Marriage Is Not for Virgins

Just recently on a clip from "The Taste," a reality show based on a cooking competition, I heard chef and author Anthony Bourdain say that a dish served to him tasted like it had been prepared by someone who had never had sex.

I applauded him for what he said.

To sample food prepared by someone who has never gone beyond salt and pepper, who has never explored how the co-mingling of sweet and savory or how the overlapping of textures can light up a diner's palate, would be a culinary bore at best.

Culinary Virgins

And the reason for such lackluster, unmemorable presentations at the dinner table is that the so-called chef has never, in any other area of her life, experienced the incredulity of being taken to a higher level, of seeing good transformed into best, or of hearing music when there are no instruments in the room.

Unaware of the existence of another reality, she settles for the guarded, mundane safety of the virginal approach, believing it is sufficient, especially if she labels it with a fancy, French name. And meanwhile, she cheats her diners out of the curried, smoked, succulent wonder they might have enjoyed, in lieu of food rivaled only by the next meal served to them by a culinary virgin.

So, for the culinary virgin, sex may be the answer.

For the would-be spouse, however, it most certainly is not.

That's because marriage is not about sex; it's about relationship. And if you enter marriage as a relationship virgin, you are in big trouble. If you wait until your wedding night to experience being fully exposed and fully accepted, you'll need I.V. Dramamine to settle you in after the rocky boat ride you'll probably have.

Long before you say, "I do," know what it is to wrestle all night with God, to be burned yet not consumed, to be disappointed and alright at the same time, to experience forgiveness you know you don't deserve, to see something truly come from absolutely nothing, to witness mountains moved and tossed into the sea, to see God far exceed anything you know how to hope for, to live in the reckless abandon of true faith, or to party with God and dance the dance of the reconciled.

. . . live in the reckless abandon of true faith, or to party with God and dance the dance of the reconciled.

Relationship Virgins

The relationship virgin knows nothing of this and is no more ready to be married than the culinary virgin is ready to be a contestant on "The Taste." She will be a marital bore and never go beyond the depth of a Lifetime movie.

Let's leave that relationship virginity at the door, where marriage is concerned, and let what you've experienced with God transform your vision of all things spicy and hot!

Taste and see that the LORD is good;
blessed is the one who takes refuge in him.
~ Psalm 34:8

Not Your Mama's Meatloaf: How Puff Pastry and Caviar Can Help You Get Your Praise On!

Recently, our family hosted three little boys from Ecuador who were invited to the United States to attend a soccer camp and to play in the Hershey Cup soccer tournament. My love for South American culture was rekindled as we talked to late hours of the night and served up as much rice and eggs as we could stand.

But at the pizzeria Friday night, little Sebas took his third and final bite of a garlic-drenched cheese slice with his eyes closed. "Es feo," he said, "pero tengo hambre." *This is disgusting, but I'm hungry.*

Holy Living—Really?

When I heard Sebas' comment, I thought of *Babette's Feast,* a film in which an entire community subsists on an unpalatable medley of boiled codfish and gruel because they assume the absence of all life's pleasantries and of all that might appeal to the senses, like color, rhythmic music, and good taste, would assure their complete devotion to God. Convinced of the impossible cohabitation of devotion and pleasure, two elderly sisters reject romance and laughter and lead their late father's congregation in a life as exciting as a piece of loose-leaf paper. And when no one expects anything better to show up on the menu, they resign themselves to: *This is disgusting, but I'm hungry.*

Then one day, the slicing of an onion, for something other than a poultice, awakens the villagers and shocks their senses into an entirely new realm. Spice enters the life of the eat-a-paper-towel club when an outsider gifts them with a sumptuous feast of delicacies they don't even have the vocabulary to describe. Quail in puff pastry and cakes with caviar and sour cream usurp the boiled codfish and gruel fare and enlighten the community palate with flavors and textures that make them raise their eyebrows and lick their spoons.

Get that Praise On!

They enjoy the deliciousness of fellowship and the hilarity of friendship as they simultaneously uncover new culinary tastes and new truths about each other. And that's when they realize the real-life analogy of that hard-to-understand reality of Jesus Christ—that in Him grace and truth exist together, side-by-side, so that they might actually kiss each other.

Efforts to bring people to a more intimate knowledge of the true and living God are empty if not somehow connected to what God has given for us to enjoy in this present life. On some level, at some time, a gift God has given for this life ought to sing a song that says, "If *this* can be so amazing, then what in the world must God be like?"

So whether we're talking about a little Ecuadorian boy who had to close his eyes to tolerate garlic pizza or whether we're talking about the congregants in *Babette's Feast* who assumed food was for fuel only, let's not assume God won't use beautiful, delicious, pleasing things that He created for us to enjoy in this world, to draw our attention to Him.

And likewise, let's not be so sure nothing better should or will ever show up on the menu . . . nor be so hungry for *something* that we settle for *anything*.

The night after the pizzeria, we made dinner for Sebas and twenty-two of his teammates. And they were really pleased with what we had for NOT-PIZZA night!

Grace and truth have met together; justice and peace have kissed each other.
~ Psalm 85:10-11

Down Broadway: Without the Neon Lights, Stardom, and Fortune

If you google *Broadway*, you get a gazillion hits about great New York City theatre, casting directors, and superstar bios.

But not long ago, a family outing took me on a ride down the other Broadway, Broadway in Brooklyn—a far cry from neon lights, stardom, and fortune. It was a sobering ride down the episodic memory lane of my life before age eight.

Violence

Greene Avenue: The house where, at age three, I sat at the kitchen table, atop two New York City telephone books, and witnessed abuse so intense that I wondered if I would have bruises just for having seen such a sight.

Death
Madison Street: Where my father and my uncle were found dead on the same night from an IV-drug overdose.

Fear
Quincy Street: Where I attended second grade and performed in the musical, *Oliver Twist,* the same year I was scared to death of being orphaned because my father was already dead.

Today as I look at my daughter, now at that same elementary age, I find myself saying, *Thank God she hasn't had to suffer any of that. I'm so glad she has no experiential context for what I felt on that family outing*.

Then I have to catch myself and remember something my husband and I have talked about a number of times—our inability to protect our precious little girl from whatever God chooses to draw her to Himself. Truthfully, I'm almost afraid to admit I understand this and that I understand it on a fairly deep level.

I would rather think of my Kaki as an uncontrolled ball of giggles and laughter who wears polka dots and stripes on Picture Day and pink and lavender on Wacky Dress Day. I don't ever want to consider what the sobering of real life issues would do to her Michael Strahan smile.

Likewise, I would never want her to enter adulthood unprepared to take a sucker punch or unable to handle disappointment. And I hate the idea of her thinking God is only powerful when no opposing forces are around. That would be a cheap facsimile of real faith in real life.

The truth of the matter is I would be a completely different person were it not for those events I was reminded of on that ride down Broadway, and without them I'd probably never find myself writing or speaking about anything meaningful.

My outer shell may reveal trauma, but my inner self, my soul, sings for my Savior—for what He did *not* withhold, for the grit through which my story shines, for my *all-rightness* despite what was clearly *not* right . . . over and over again.

My outer shell may reveal trauma, but my inner self, my soul, sings for my Savior—for what He did *not* withhold, for the grit through which my story shines, for my *all-rightness* despite what was clearly not right . . . over and over again.

From the Lord comes deliverance . . .
~ Psalm 3:8

When You Don't Get a Do-Over

Ever been afraid of telling it like it is? Afraid of telling the truth because the would-be recipient was older, more experienced, or somehow more important than you were? After all, the old are supposed to lead the young, right? I know the feeling well, but one day God squeezed it out of me in a way that left His handprints all over me ever since.

My grandfather, Theodore Roosevelt Williams, once a robust man with a hearty, contagious laugh, lay stretched out in comatose silence in his hospital bed, wearing an oversized, steel blue gown that hung sloppily off his skeletal torso. The dingy, white piping around the top was tied loosely in a bow that rested on his emaciated neck. He was unrecognizable, and that devastated me.

The Memory
I was used to seeing Grandpop, sitting comfortably in a recliner, telling funny stories about working with his brothers down at the Brooklyn waterfront.

I wanted to hear him laugh again. I wanted him to bet me that he could eat a whole loaf of Profile bread in one sitting, without once forgetting to dunk a piece in his coffee. I wanted to see him sharpen his razor on a leather barber's strap and slick his hair back with Vitalis. I wanted him to give me a roll of peppermint Lifesavers and send me on my way as he did every single time I saw him. I wanted to make him another Father's Day card as I had done every year since first grade when my father died.

The Reality
But there he lay in a coma, so lifeless. I felt unprepared for all this. I had been away at college, and so I had not seen his gradual decline in weight and wellness. Someone told me that I should talk to him because there was a good chance that he could hear me even if he didn't respond.

Well, I thought, *I certainly have plenty I could tell him.* I had gotten saved, that he already knew, but the spiritual growth, the sense of being led to the mission field—that would have truly excited him.

But the words never came. I could have gone step-by-step through the gospel, making sure he had no doubts as to how to be saved, but I said nothing. I sat there paralyzed in silence, apparently overcome by this "imposter" in my grandfather's bed with tubes in his nose and an IV in his arm.

The Cowardice

Instead of saying something, I glanced out the window, and I saw one of my cousins entering the hospital. I didn't want to be seen as emotionally overcome as I was, so I decided it was time for me to leave. About a week later, when I was back at school, my mother called to say that Grandpop had passed away. My heart broke into a thousand pieces. Somehow, I thought God would have spared him. I wasn't even sure if I felt that way because I truly wanted him well or because I truly wanted another shot at doing what I was too cowardly to do when I saw him in person.

What was wrong with me? This was my Grandpop. I held the keys to the kingdom, but I was too afraid to open my mouth. And what was I afraid of? Of being laughed at? Of someone else overhearing me? Of losing my position as "favorite" granddaughter because I dared to wonder whether or not he really did know Christ as Savior?

Would God really let *him* go to hell because *I* didn't have the courage to speak up? So then, I was preparing to go to the ends of the earth to share the gospel but not to Downstate Medical Center in Brooklyn? Not to my own grandfather?

At his funeral, I realized I had never allowed myself to consider Grandpop's eventual death. How I wished I could relive that day in the hospital, that I could open my mouth and say what the redeemed of the Lord say. I needed the Lord to comfort my heart in a way that no one else could at that time. I asked Him for a verse, and He gave me Mark 7:37: "...He has done all things well . . ."

I've always taken that to mean: Even when Sherry disappoints, even when Sherry fails miserably . . . God does all things well.

Jesus urged them to keep it quiet but they talked it up all the more, beside themselves with excitement. 'He's done it all and done it well . . . '
~ Mark 7:37, *The Message*

The Taboo Test: Engage Your Audience with What You Do *Not* Say

The geniuses at Hasbro had the right idea when they came up with a party game that had players shouting, laughing, interrupting each other, thinking with their arms and fists, and jumping to their feet.

They published the game, *Taboo, the* most engaging game I've ever played and one I'd highly recommend as a warm-up exercise for any writer or speaker who wants their God-given message embedded in the hearts and on the tongue tips of all who encounter it.

The Game

In the game a player chooses a card with a word or phrase at the top, like *chef* and several "taboo" words underneath that top word, such as "*hat, food,* *restaurant, cook,* and *make."** The object of the game is for the player to get her team to say *chef* without the player using the word *chef,* the taboo words, or any forms of those words, including those that rhyme.

So instead of resorting to the expected, stale description of "chef" which would be something like, "The guy who cooks your food at a restaurant," the player is forced to use something unexpected and fresh like, "The artist who creates your braised veal ribs with caramelized shallots."

Both the player who comes up with the unique word picture and the one who deciphers it and shouts, "Chef!" before anyone else experience a certain satisfaction, having been carried away to an infinitely more fun and interesting place than the "guy who cooks . . . " scenario might have led.

The Test

When you write or prepare to speak, consider your topic and quickly jot down everything that first comes to mind in relation to it. Thirty seconds later when you examine your list, you'll probably have a grouping of the most predictable, yawn-inducing, circa 1990 approaches to your topic, clichés and all.

Next, eliminate everything on that list and anything that may subsequently occur to you that rhymes with Adam and Eve or that encourages one to compare trusting God to sitting in a chair. Offensive and antiquated don't go far enough to describe those approaches in this century.

You can use this same process as a test for material you've already written or presented; just go back and tweak before using it again.

Determine to use another approach to your topic that won't have your audience rolling their eyes, guessing your next sentence as they read, or lip-syncing your talk because they've heard it all before.

Make Them Shout, "Jesus!"
How can you do that?

Well, let's say you were writing about your Savior. Now imagine the name "Jesus" at the top of your *Taboo* game card. And imagine that the unmentionable taboo words included God, son, Messiah, cross, blood, Bible, Joseph, Mary, died, sin, and every other word or term that a textbook explanation of Jesus might include.

What better chance is there for you, whose ministry it is to make His name known to your audience—the players, than to make them shout, "Jesus!" when you say, "The silencer of my critics," "the giver of fourth trimesters," "the champion of second chances," or "the voice of the mute"?

Cause them to see your Jesus with 3-D glasses and from the inside out.

And leave the *Taboo* words where they belong—on a card in a game box.

Let the redeemed of the Lord say so.
~ Psalm 107:2

*This card actually appears as one of thousands offered in the database of the Taboo game online at http://taboogame.net/

The Sound of My Faith: A Song for Those Who Feel They Don't Belong

O to be swept into worship
With that rhythmic gospel
That my soul longs to offer back to my God.
For it is He who has made my heart
To beat to the very music of His Word
And who has made my feet dance
To the celebration of His goodness and glory.
Great, grand voices that dig deeply into each word,
Proclaiming and celebrating a personal encounter with the King of kings
Despite daily struggles with the prince of darkness,
Scrape the sod off my heavy, downtrodden spirit,
And in a renewed lightness, with each crescendo,
I clap my hands even louder in amen agreement.
If I try to contain the song that is on my lips
When I hear of the many things "written aforetime for our learning,"
The very tears of my eyes cry out in protest,

For it is *He* who has created me
And the sound of my faith.

He who has created me
And the sound of my faith
Has sent me to a foreign land
To be swept into worship with a sweet, strange melody
In which my soul struggles to find release.
My heart searches for and my feet seek that which is muzzled
In a quieter, more subdued proclamation of truth, and so
In my heart I run to and fro,
Desperately looking for a way, a place, a means to celebrate.
And then it hits me.
This *is* my portion.
My heart must beat silently to the music of His Word.
My feet must dance within shoes that are laced and bound.
When my downtrodden yet redeemed soul is scraped clean and given hope
By the "patience and comfort of the Scriptures," I will not dare to shout "Amen,"
For my tongue will be bound.
I will not clap, for my hands will be stilled.
The tears of my eyes protest inwardly,
For this is my portion.
Shall I then cease to desire to be swept into that rhythmic gospel
That my soul longs to offer back to my God?
No, no, no, not ever!

For it is *He* who has created me
And the sound of my faith.

Shout for joy to the LORD, all the earth. Worship the LORD with gladness; come before him with joyful songs.
~ Psalm 100:1, 2

Redeeming the Sound of My Faith: A Song of Praise and Deliverance for Those Who Have at Some Time Awakened to Find Themselves Clapping When There Was No Music

O to be swept into worship
With that rhythmic gospel
That my soul longs to offer back to my God.
For it is He who has made my heart
To beat to the very music of His Word
And who has made my feet dance
To the celebration of His goodness and glory.
Great, grand voices that dig deeply into each word,
Proclaiming and celebrating a personal encounter with the King of kings
Despite daily struggles with the prince of darkness,
Scrape the sod off my heavy, downtrodden spirit,
And in a renewed lightness, with each crescendo,
I clap my hands even louder in amen agreement.

If I try to contain the song that is on my lips
When I hear of the many things "written aforetime for our learning,"
The very tears of my eyes cry out in protest,
For it is *He* who created me
And the sound of my faith.

He who created me
And the sound of my faith
Has sent me to a foreign land
To be swept into worship with a sweet, strange melody
In which my soul struggles to find release.
My heart searches for and my feet seek that which is muzzled
In a quieter, more subdued proclamation of truth, and so
In my heart I run to and fro,
Desperately looking for a way, a place, a means to celebrate.
And then it hits me.
This *is* my portion.
But shall *my* heart beat silently to the music of His Word?
Shall *my* feet cease to dance within my shoes?
When my downtrodden yet redeemed soul is scraped clean and given hope
By the "patience and comfort of the Scriptures," I will indeed shout, "Amen!"
For my tongue will not be bound.
I will indeed clap, for my hands will not be stilled.
I will learn to rejoice in this, my portion.
Shall I, therefore, still desire to be swept into that rhythmic gospel

That my soul longs to offer back to my God?
Yes, yes, yes, forever!
For it is *He* who created me
And the sound of my faith.

Know that the LORD is God. It is he who made us, and we are his; we are his people, the sheep of his pasture.
~ Psalm 100: 3

Honest Abe, Geico, and How You Can Know if You're Ready for Marriage

A couple of years ago my husband and I saw a commercial for Geico auto insurance which dramatizes a supposed conversation between Abraham Lincoln and his wife. A short, rotund Mary Todd Lincoln primps in front of a mirror, straightens and examines her high-neck, lace-cuffed, derriere-spreading black and white taffeta dress from different angles, and then asks that dreaded question:

"Honey, does this dress make my backside look big?"

Was Abraham Lincoln Honest?

Honest Abe is caught in a quandary.

I could almost hear the tug-of-war in his head. Shouldn't I always be truthful with my wife? Would it really be better for me to lie and risk the chance of someone else telling her the truth? If she knows I love her, who cares about some silly dress? Do I even mention that when we met I guessed her age by sizing up her girth, in the same way some determine the age of a tree by counting its rings?

Poor guy.

He summons up enough nerve to break the news to her and even enough cool to say it sweetly. Clearly, the last thing on earth he wants to do is hurt her feelings or provoke her to what many historians refer to as Mary Todd Lincoln's bipolar episodes.

Is Honesty the Best Policy?

"Maybe just the tiniest little bit," he says while pantomiming exactly what you picture in your mind when someone says "teeny-weeny."

> One night my husband took me aside and said, "You need an intervention."

Full of disdain, and perhaps a Twinkie or two too many, Mrs. Lincoln storms off in a tizzy, insulted that her husband would say such a thing to her.

Such an unreasonable excuse for a wife, I thought—that is, until it happened to me.

And my scenario wasn't nearly as bad as hers.

Let me explain.

I Need a What?
One night my husband took me aside and said, "You need an intervention."

"A what?" I asked.

"An I-N-T-E-R-V-E-N-T-I-O-N," he enunciated like an ESL teacher.

I'm Not Ready to Be Okay with This!
My very first response was to pull a Mary Todd Lincoln. I put on my Brooklyn-girl-with-an-attitude face, rolled my eyes, put my hands on my hips, and inhaled so that I could tongue-lash and tie him up all in one breath.

But before I could say something intentionally hurtful like, "Hey, if we're talking about looks here, you ain't exactly stoppin' traffic," I heard the tail end of something that ended in, "You're beautiful."

I was disarmed.

What my husband had said was, "Please don't think this has anything to do with how *you* look—you're beautiful." Then he continued, saying, "It's just that lately you've been dressing overly casual at some not-so-casual affairs. You have such good things to share with people. I'd just hate to see it all overlooked because of how you're dressed."

Don't you hate it when nice guys say something potentially lethal in such a nice way that they're even nicer for having said it?

And as I pictured myself the last few months at special events over the holidays, I did indeed spot myself in sweatpants, oversized sweaters, and even a tattered t-shirt I wore backwards because the holes were less noticeable that way—all at the most inopportune times.

I'm really glad for that intervention, and especially for a husband who loves me enough to tell me the truth without tearing me down or attaching it to my self-worth.

But please take this as a warning: There are lots of interventions in healthy marriages. If there aren't, then one or both partners is spending a lot of time bound and gagged, with their heads in the sand, or just downright lying.

So, if truth-telling puts you more at ease than up in arms and if you think Mary Todd Lincoln is just a tad annoying in this scenario, you are well on your way to being ready for marriage!

Therefore each of you must put off falsehood and speak truthfully to your neighbor, for we are all members of one body.
~ Ephesians 4:25

What Do *Finding Nemo, The Lion King,* and Your Life Have in Common?

They are all wonderful illustrations of redemption told through story. In each case, someone orphaned or lost is pursued with great fervor until he is brought back to where he should be and to where his primary relationship or purpose is restored.

In *Finding Nemo,* a young fish's disobedience causes him to be swept away, far from his home. He lands in increasingly dangerous dilemmas while his father searches everywhere for him, and they are ultimately reunited.

In *The Lion King,* young Simba loses his father and loses his way until his father speaks to him from on high to remind him of his ultimate purpose in life. And *your* life? Well, *that* story you already know.

The most radical things God teaches us in his Word are taught through story. And that's probably because we, the presumptuous, over-truthed, grace-proof, doers of the law, wouldn't quite GET it any other way.

An entirely different idea of what God is like emerges when I read, "Do not lie," from Exodus 20, than when I read how God handles Rahab's lying frenzy in Joshua 2, or the lying of the "righteous" Ananias and Sapphira in Acts 5.

These stories demonstrate how God cares a whole lot more about the condition of our hearts than what might slip off our tongues.

That same thing happens when I read "God is love" without any context, versus reading it alongside the story of Hosea, who loved and pursued his wife throughout her horrendous acts of harlotry. Who in the world does something like that?

Without the benefit of story our idea of God gets in the way of the truth of God, and what we end up with is a mistaken image of a god who fits nicely within our finite, intellectual, spirit-devoid grasp.

So, what story will you tell? What's your *Finding Nemo* or *The Lion King*? How will you describe a God who is powerful enough to split the Red Sea, cause the sun to stand still, and raise a dead man from his grave, but sensitive and caring enough to pursue us, forgive us, and love us before we've ever even acknowledged who He is?

You did not choose me, but I chose you and appointed you so that you might go and bear fruit . . .
~ John 15:16

Why You Should Never March Down the Aisle Unless You're Already Married

For your Maker is your husband—the Lord Almighty is His name."

There it was, plain as day.

Isaiah 54:5.

A verse so steeped in nuptial goodness I could hardly read it without a swatch of tulle hanging from my head—the verse that encouraged me to have an impromptu wedding ceremony as I flew to the Peruvian Amazon for the first time.

I was a new missionary, still somewhat disappointed that I wasn't beginning that new chapter with a husband.

Then I realized that wasn't true! I *was* beginning that journey with a husband, and not just in an allegorical sense.

Here Comes the Bride!

I was dead serious. With a ring I bought from a gift shop in Panama during my layover, my Bible, and my vows, I declared myself the bride of Christ so definitively that I knew any earthly mate God might one day give would have to understand that he was my second husband, and the first one wasn't going away.

What God Hath Joined Together . . .

I was a happy wife until, somewhere along the way, the fact of *my* husband being *your* husband, and *her* husband, and the husband of all who read Isaiah 54:5 became a little unsettling.

And pardon the revisiting of my New York City roots, but didn't that make God a two-timer? And a two-timer a zillion times over?

I wanted exclusivity.

And, yes, though I knew God was big enough to handle me and anyone else in the universe, there was something bittersweet and polygamous about having to share my intimate partner with every Tallulah, Jane, and Ally.

Then God settled my angst.

He Loves *Me*!

One weekend on a twenty-six hour ride on a public Amazon River launch, I curled up in my hammock, decidedly ignoring the stench, gawks and squeals of animals around me, and the swing-swish-foot-brushing of people below me, took out my Bible, and got down to doing business with God.

I was good and ready—not exactly *mad,* but fully-armed with what I knew were formidable inquiries as to what in the world God was doing in my life.

My co-workers, a Peruvian couple from Lima, had travelled back to the capital for medical treatments. It looked as though the wife may have had breast cancer, and there was no available treatment for that in the jungle where we were.

I was afraid of losing a great friend, and their weeks-long trip left me to do our church-planting work alone in our village for an extended period. It seemed that much of what I did at that time became increasingly isolating. For short stays someone might travel with me or come upriver to help with a particular program or something, but they'd all eventually go back to what they previously did.

And so on that particular day, on the heaviest day of my cycle, after getting neck to toe and backpack soaked falling into the river while boarding a launch to go twenty-six hours without a bathroom I could fit into, preparing to speak at a retreat at the end of those twenty-six hours, and as lonely as lonely could be, I felt a little bit picked on.

Why would I give you away to someone else when I don't fully have you myself?

I gave it to the Lord . . . all in one breath . . .

Lord, aren't I okay with you? I love you, I serve you every day, and I even drink masato till it gets stuck in my teeth. Why, then, can't I have what I really want? Why can't I have what I have been asking for? Why can't I have a permanent ministry partner?*

Just then, at the ceremonial ringing of the launch's dinner bell—just before the swing-swish-foot-brushing turned into a wild run for arroz con frijoles,* the Lord spoke to my heart so clearly that He may as well have said it out loud: *Why would I give you away to someone else when I don't fully have you myself?*

I never once wondered if I understood Him correctly, never once imagined what smart-alecky response I might offer to the One who knew me better than I knew myself.

He wanted me to know that in all my *missionary-ing* I had forgotten Him, my husband—the One to whom I was betrothed as I flew to the Peruvian Amazon.

And *He* missed *me*. My husband, the King of the universe, my Savior, missed me and wanted me to be fully connected to Him before ever extending my hand to anyone else in marriage.

Suddenly, I didn't care about Tallulah, Jane, or Ally because I knew no other soul in the universe had *my* particular relationship—my marriage with *my* Savior.

And I had my exclusivity.

For your Maker is your husband—the Lord Almighty is his name.
~ Isaiah 54:5

*Masato is a thick drink made from cooked yucca that is chewed, spit out, and fermented.

*Arroz con frijoles is rice with beans.

Five Godly Things God Doesn't Want You to Do

Make a joyful noise to the Lord (Psalm 100:1-2)
. . . without addressing the unrighteous outburst you splattered over your eight-year-old for acting like a second grader.

Preach the Word (2 Timothy 4:2)
. . . before you've loaded the dishwasher for Grandma Sally.

Esteem others better than Yourself (Philippians 2:3)
. . . when it's only because you want them to bolster your own image.

Hide His Word in your heart (Psalm 119:11)

. . . just so you can look like a big shot in the eyes of others.

Be ready to defend your faith (I Peter 3:15)
. . . in order to humiliate unbelievers who you think should grovel to the cross in shame.

What good is it, my brothers and sisters, if someone claims to have faith but has no deeds? Can such faith save them? Suppose a brother or sister is without clothes and daily food. If one of you says to them, "Go in peace; keep warm and well fed," but does nothing about their physical needs, what good is it? In the same way, faith by itself, if it is not accompanied by action, is dead.
~ James 2:14-17

For All You *Les Miserables* Groupies

Every once in a while I jump in my car, roll up the windows to create that perfect "surround-sound," and blast my favorite songs from the original soundtrack of the Broadway musical, *Les Miserables,* based on Victor Hugo's novel by the same name.

And each time I find myself overwhelmed with such clear themes of law, grace, forgiveness, and redemption.

Origin of the Lyrics

What's interesting, though, is that it seems neither Victor Hugo, the novelist, nor Herbert Kretzmer, the writer of the English language lyrics for *Les Miserables,* the musical, tried to talk Bible when they crafted this story.

Instead, they both wrote from their interactions with man's inhumanity to man and with the endless struggles of outcasts and underdogs at the hands of the righteous.

Hugo did so from his social and political experiences in nineteenth century France just after the French Revolution, and Kretzmer wrote from his years growing up in South Africa, "a country that had more than its share of the righteous hurrying past and not seeing what was happening around them." (Herbert Kretzmer in his interview with Al Sheahen for *The Barricade*, the in-house magazine of *Les Miserables* companies around the world, 1998..)

The God of It

How awe-inspiring that God uses things we hate, situations that frustrate us, and those times that truly try our souls, to bring us to the same conclusions I suspect He would rather us come to much more easily.

But we don't.

And so the fire comes.

Disappointment. Devastation. Loss. Injustice. Humiliation.

For me, frustration builds and backs me up against the fence until I have nothing left. The only choice that remains is to beg God for help—to turn my attention to Him where it should have been all along.

Who Needs God?

But sooner or later, I have to put on my Big Girl Spanks and just say what is true: Who in the world needs God to be happy in a life devoid of disappointment, devastation, loss, injustice or humiliation?

> I can love people who love me, ignore people who hate me, talk about people who I think are different, and declare all to be godly when I have a righteous majority of people who agree with me—all quite easily without God, thank you.

How hard can that be?

Who needs help to do what comes naturally?

I don't. . . . I can love people who love me, ignore people who hate me, talk about people who I think are different, and declare all to be godly when I have a righteous majority of people who agree with me—all quite easily without God, thank you.

But what happens when my righteous little world is shaken by real-life dilemmas, when I am blamed for what I have not done or cannot change, when I am called to forgive when I am the victim and my perpetrator runs free, when I am drowning because the unrelenting waves are bigger than I am, when I realize there is always someone for whom I will never be good enough?

I believe Hugo and Kretzmer would say these are all universal experiences of life.

If I let go of myself and reach for God, then even in my *un-rightness* I am all right. And it is my *all-rightness,* despite what is clearly *not* right, that turns people's attention to God. This is the outworking of Matthew 5:16 in everyday real life:

. . . Let your light shine before others, that they may see your good deeds and glorify your Father in heaven.
~ Matthew 5:16

Why Chicken Soup Doesn't Always Cure Colds

Okay, there's that sore spot again.

You know how you press your big toe against the inside of your shoe over and over again when you have an ingrown toenail—presumably because you need to be sure the nail is still there and still causing pain?

Well, that's what I've done for the umpteenth time now with gazillions of articles out there supposedly designed to help single women find a match; I keep reading them!

And I keep screaming.

And in my frustration I read more.

The dumbing down of real life issues has led a lot of sincere people to conclude that a woman's singleness MUST be a result of her desperation, her inability to roll with the punches, or with her insistence that her man has a J-O-B and a street address that differs from his mother's.

Maybe writing a book on marriage drives me to this crazy irritation. Or maybe it's living on a campus, where girls feel like failures if they don't order their wedding invitations at the same time as their graduation announcements, that does it. Or maybe dating twenty years before finding my Mr. Right has put me over the edge.

But, just for the record, I'm a little sensitive about how the married world views the "condition" of the single woman.

What if a woman is single because God wants her single?

Or because He knows she would hate married life?

Or because He has something so monumental for her to do that mixing it with the mundane would be almost funny?

Or because He's trying to cut her a break?

Or because He wants her to know He is as much a comforter as people with skin are?

Or because He wants to spare her the pain of losing a man?

Or because the one thing everyone knows Jane Doe can't do without is a man . . . Then she doesn't get one . . . and somehow Jane is fine with that.

Who, then, gets the glory?

Marriage doesn't always solve problems any more than chicken soup always cures colds.

Nevertheless, each person should live as a believer in whatever situation the Lord has assigned to them, just as God has called them.
~ I Corinthians 7:17

Is It Your Fault Your Kids Don't GET Christ?

Even if you don't have kids or even if you're not parenting teens or young adults, if you are in any way influential in the life of someone in this category, read on . . .

First, let's think about how we handle their sin. And if we're talking about blatant sin, caught red-handed, we'd have to be crazy to ignore what Jesus did when the teachers of religious law and the Pharisees—the long-robed, Holier than Thou Club—brought to Him a woman caught in the act of adultery in John 8:3-11.

Jesus is seated in the temple courts surrounded by a crowd He is about to teach when the "Club" shows up with this woman whose sin they are sure will command swift and severe punishment. They shame her to stand before the group as they announce their discovery to Jesus:

“Teacher, this woman was caught in the act of adultery. In the Law Moses commanded us to stone such a woman. Now what do you say?”

In one of the biggest rush-to-judgment moments in history, the Club is certain it has successfully condemned a woman to a death she deserves while successfully trapping Jesus, the Giver of grace, into agreeing with them or being discredited by the crowd.

It doesn’t work.

What happens next surprises many who are present just as it surprises many who read this account today.

“ . . . Jesus bent down and started to write on the ground with his finger. When they kept on questioning him, he straightened up and said to them, ‘If any one of you is without sin, let him be the first to throw a stone at her.’ Again he stooped down and wrote on the ground.”

Let’s Call It What It Is

We don't know what Jesus writes on the ground in this passage, but we do know that, coupled with His admonition for anyone without sin to be the first to cast a stone, it radically changes the scene from a dog fight to a recessional.

Jesus brings the so-called righteous to a revolutionary understanding of their own sin—not the generic, universal sin we all bear as human beings descended from Adam, but a revelation of their specific brand of arrogance that proves they aren't who they think they are.

What Jesus does removes the smell of meat from the noses of hungry dogs and causes the previously drooling accusers to march away with their tails between their legs.

That's what He does for the accusers.

Resist the Condemnation Chorus

For the adulterer Jesus asks, "Where are they? Has no one condemned you?" To which she responds, "No one, sir." And then that great redemptive moment: "Then neither do I condemn you. Go now, and leave your life of sin."

> It's that moment we should all pray for—that moment when God causes the sinner to be irresistibly drawn to the cross because she knows the stench of transgression on her breath alone reveals her guilt, yet she is pardoned.

No sugar-coating the fact of her sin, but no condemnation chorus either. Does a woman brought forth to be stoned need to be told what she deserves for her sin?

Just Forgive

It's that moment we should all pray for—that moment when God causes the sinner to be irresistibly drawn to the cross because she knows the stench of transgression on her breath alone reveals her guilt, yet she is pardoned.

Her accusers walk away silenced by their recently-exposed sin, but the adulteress remains—face to face with Jesus, fully revealed, and yet fully embraced.

Drop the Shame Game

Forgiveness and grace seep out from the seams of this story. Not truth. And that's not because truth is unimportant but because, apparently, everyone in this scenario was already well aware of the truth.

For Jesus to use this opportunity to remind the woman that she shouldn't have been committing adultery would be counterproductive. The whole idea of being "caught" implies a degree of hiding to begin with. So is she unaware of her sin? Is she unclear that her only hope of escape from the penalty of adultery is the miraculous intervention of Jesus?

Are we who struggle with our weight unaware that we'll soon be squeezing through front doors sideways? Are we unclear that our only hope of escape from the penalty of overeating is the miraculous intervention of Spanks?

So what do you do when your kids are caught in the act of sin? Do you drag them in front of their peers, announce their sin, and hope their public humiliation and shame will summon back-pats and cheers for you, the righteous, who scarcely would have thought of such filth? Do you help the would-be executors of justice gather their stones?

Or do you recall your own sin—that debauchery for which you still struggle to believe God forgave you—for which you secretly wish you could recompense with myriad good works?

And do you think, *this may be my one chance to BE Christ to my children—to forgive them now when the seriousness of their sin has heightened their understanding of depravity and has caused them to relinquish all hope from ever being right with God or with me?*

And do you do it simply because it is what God, in Christ, did for you? And do you anticipate their being irresistibly drawn to the cross because they realize they'd never be able to earn what they were just given so freely?

Never let it be said that when your kids are caught red-handed in sin, the biggest reason they don't ever have a change of heart is because you're too busy gathering stones.

Be kind and compassionate to one another, forgiving each other, just as in Christ God forgave you.
~ Ephesians 4:32

Why I'm Still Married and What That Could Mean for You

Each year on Valentine's Day I celebrate the anniversary of my husband singing to me Steven Curtis Chapman's "I Will Be Here" and asking the greatest rhetorical question imaginable:

Will you marry me?

He says I never actually answered him, and I say attitude, body language, and decibel level should have been enough. On that day, fifteen years ago, I still had a lot to learn about Ted, the Grace-a-holic-I Have to Pass Every Possible Scenario Through My Mind Before Responding-Boykin. I'm amazed at how much good sisterly advice did for me in those early years. Maybe it will do the same for you.

Left Brain/Right Brain

Early in our marriage, it was all about putting my first reactions aside and giving my husband the benefit of the doubt. He's one of those deep thinkers who conceives ideas in his flowery, sensitive right brain but who expresses those ideas through his matter-of-fact, pragmatic left brain.

And, on top of that, there's usually an uncomfortably long pause after he begins to express himself (presumably when he realizes the potential harm in what he has already said), followed by a brief fixer-upper statement. It usually goes something like this:

After I married my wife, I realized she was nothing like the woman I thought I married . . . (super long pause) . . . I realized she was so much more.

I'll Kill Him!

Feeling my pain? For at least seven of our fourteen years of marriage I bit my tongue, curled my toes, and plotted his death through those "super long pauses." I often felt insulted or hurt. Giving my husband the benefit of the doubt was something I had to do intentionally—like putting a block on channel fifty-eight to avoid watching C-SPAN by accident when I was too lazy to get up and get the remote.

Now, all these years later, I don't even tune into the highly-ignitable stuff that precedes those long pauses. I just perk up my ears to make sure I don't miss the heart of my husband in what he says after the pauses.

And I'm usually glad I did.

Also, you should probably know that those uncomfortably long pauses between awkward statements and heartfelt, fuzzy words often extend past his speech and into his physical reactions to obvious stimuli.

Case in point: One day as I muscled a bag of heavy props out of the elevator on my way to teach a class, I saw my husband down the hallway walking and talking with one of his students. I perked up and waved at him like a ten-year-old.

No reaction.

I waved a second time when I was sure he saw me, only this time I stretched higher and shook my hand twice as fast.

Still no reaction.

My old friend, "Benefit of the Doubt," kicked in.

Am I Invisible?
What's his problem? I know he's legally blind, but with glasses his eyesight is corrected to eagle vision, quickly gave way to, I don't get this, but I'm guessing there's some reasonable explanation for it.

I went into the classroom, literally pictured myself taking this bothersome little issue and throwing it in the trash, then greeted my class.

A minute or two later, my husband walked in the classroom and gave me a big hug and kiss. He said he was praying for me because he knew from our conversation that morning that I felt nervous and anxious about teaching that day.

So why didn't he wave back?

Arthritis?

Who knows? But I'll take a hug and a kiss over a wave anytime.

Try it!

. . . Rather, in humility value others above yourselves, not looking to your own interests but each of you to the interests of the others.
~ Philippians 2:3, 4

A Lesson from My Seven-Year-Old: The Family Recipe

My seven-year-old daughter and I watched our favorite cooking show one day in preparation for the Fourth of July. The show featured a chef who had built a catering business and a restaurant, inspired by his grandfather's recipe of a toe-curling barbecue sauce that sounded like you couldn't even taste it properly without taking off your shoes.

Kaki and I wanted that recipe. We anticipated something that would compel us to eat a Frisbee if it were marinated long enough; after all, we were talking about *Memphis BBQ,* right?

Before his great revelation, the BBQ chef admitted he was confused as to why his businesses hadn't really soared like he thought they would—why he didn't have people holding him hostage for that family recipe.

He called a mentor chef for help. But when the mentor said he didn't like the sauce, the BBQ chef just stared at him. There was no way anyone was going to tell him his family recipe wasn't gold.

Then came the showdown. The BBQ chef was ready to tell the mentor how he made his special sauce, and he was ready to prove that something was wrong with the mentor's palate if he wasn't slapping himself after eating it.

"Mommy?" she asked as if her world just stopped spinning. "Is he saying he made barbecue sauce out of *barbecue sauce?*"

Shockingly and unashamedly, the BBQ chef plunked down a gallon-size bottle of his local supermarket's BBQ sauce along with three or four other ingredients, which I believe included ketchup and mustard.

Huh?

Even my seven-year-old had to catch her jaw before it hit the floor.

"Mommy?" she asked as if her world just stopped spinning. "Is he saying he made barbecue sauce out of *barbecue sauce?*"

Still unbelieving myself, I shook my head. "I guess so, honey."

In the sixteen years that chef had in the BBQ business, I'll bet he had opportunities to come up with some pretty innovative ideas and recipes. Nevertheless, his creative juices were limited to doctoring up an already-made product—someone else's stuff.

This stands in such contrast to God who created the world out of absolutely nothing. Read Genesis 1 and 2 for yourself.

He didn't spawn you, the zebra, or the mighty oak from Og and Blob floating around in Precambrian water.

No.

He crafted you, formed the zebra and painted its stripes, and raised up the mighty oak and all the intricacies of the world without pre-existent DNA or anything else.

You were made in the image of God, and you too are creative. Just ask Him to help you get those creative juices flowing. It may take a while, and it may not be easy, but don't ever settle for someone else's stuff when you're making your family recipe.

Let's depend on the One who doesn't need barbecue sauce to come up with . . . barbecue sauce.

In the beginning God created the heavens and the earth.
~ Genesis 1:1

Mr. Wonderful

Let me tell you about my Mr. Wonderful: incredible, intelligent, and interested in me! His ministry as a Christian counselor honed his feminine understanding skills so much that I envied him myself. And it didn't hurt that he flashed a big, Pepsodent-white grin and raced around in a red sports car.

Mutual friends introduced us after he saw my picture at their house and asked about me. We were acquainted by phone five months before he drove from the Southeast to the Midwest to join me for a weekend singles' retreat.

Mr. Wonderful and I hit it off at the retreat, and, soon afterwards, a plane ticket arrived in the mail along with an invite to spend Thanksgiving with MW (Mr. Wonderful) and his family. I packed twelve outfits for four days and got my hair freeze-curled so tightly that my Sharpie got stuck in it when I tapped the side of my head. I had to sleep upside down with my head hanging off the bed to keep my coif from losing its "natural" symmetry—the perfect formula for optimal cuteness.

MW's family, the southern Huxtables, were a dream, but something happened during Thanksgiving dinner. While I rejoiced that no one plopped a chitlin' on my plate, MW became increasingly quiet and withdrawn. Each time I asked what was wrong, he interrupted with, "Uh, well, um . . . guess I'll explain later."

The strange behavior continued through the weekend until my Sunday afternoon flight. We agreed to go two weeks without contacting each other so MW could grow enough courage to speak his mind.

The two weeks ended on my birthday, and MW called. Thirty seconds into the "Um, well . . ." routine, he confessed, "I really like you, but I've always seen myself going out with someone . . . pretty."

I sat there, a live volcano ready to spew its lava. I rumbled and shook before a single word came forth. Then I erupted and burned MW with molten words so fiery that no amount of water would ever quench them.

I hung up.

"I really like you, but I've always seen myself going out with someone . . . pretty."

I cried.

And when I looked in the mirror, I saw ugly. When I looked past the glare in a store window, I saw ugly. Why? Because MW had declared me to be so.

I took all the mirrors out of my apartment, removed all the bright lights, and lived in darkness for three whole years.

Then the real Mr. Wonderful went to battle for my heart—not the MW who shattered me but the One who pursued me, piece by piece, to make me whole again. Since I refused to look in the mirror, He caused me to see my true reflection in His Word.

Psalm 139:14, ". . . I am fearfully and wonderfully made . . ." was on the radio whenever I listened. It was preached from the pulpit on more Sundays than seemed reasonable, and it was part of virtually every testimony I heard at that time.

Little by little, the lights came on again. I replaced the mirrors and scotch-taped that verse to every one of them. I did the same for the walls, the doors, the dashboard of my car, and my desk at work. *I am fearfully and wonderfully made . . . I am fearfully and wonderfully made . . . I am fearfully and wonderfully made!*

Even on days when I had no desire to do so, I forced myself to look in the mirror and recite that verse over and over again until the Lord eventually renewed my soul with it, just like silver polish dissolves tarnish and a little scrubbing wipes it away.

I was beautiful because the real Mr. Wonderful—my Lord and my Creator God—the One who had fashioned me according to His liking and who had eyes to see what no man could see, had declared me to be so.

I praise you because I am fearfully and wonderfully made; your works are wonderful, I know that full well.
~ Psalm 139:14

The Face I've Earned

My husband and I laughed our bottoms off one night as we watched a commercial advertising the services of a local plastic surgeon. The spokeswoman in the commercial gave a lengthy discussion about procedures using collagen, Botox, facial implants, etc., and she explained it all without ever moving her upper lip—not because she didn't want to but, apparently, because she couldn't. A little too much of something had rendered her upper lip immovable!

You should know that I honestly believe in doing the best you can with what you have. I just wonder if some women are going too far.

One of the article headlines in a recent edition of *Good Housekeeping* was entitled, "Woman Avoids Smiling for 40 Years to Stop Wrinkles." The woman is quoted as saying, "My dedication paid off. I don't have a single line on my face."[1]

Is it really so bad to have laugh lines that map the way back to hilarious experiences you've had? That let people know you're a kid at heart? That give testimony of a God who gives the gift of laughter even after unmentionable pain?

Huh?

Not one little giggle out at that pizza place with her friends? Nary a chuckle during a funny movie? No school-girl grin at the altar? Not even a proud-mama smile when her child said something immeasurably cute?

All that to have the "pleasure" of being asked if she'd had Botox treatments once she reached age fifty?

How sad.

Is it really so bad to have laugh lines that map the way back to hilarious experiences you've had? That let people know you're a kid at heart? That give testimony of a God who gives the gift of laughter even after unmentionable pain?

---

[1]Marlisse Cepeda. "Woman Avoids Smiling for 40 Years to Stop Wrinkles." *Good Housekeeping.* Posted February 4, 2015. http://www.goodhousekeeping.com/beauty/anti-aging/tips/a26554/woman-avoids-smiling-40-years/.

I was blessed to have a baby at age forty-three. Somehow, I got through that without a single stretch mark.

I really wish I had gotten one.

And I kind of wish it were across my face.

The righteous will flourish like a palm tree, they will grow like a cedar of Lebanon; planted in the house of the LORD, they will flourish in the courts of our God. They will still bear fruit in old age, they will stay fresh and green, proclaiming, "The LORD is upright; he is my Rock, and there is no wickedness in him."

~ Psalm 92:12-15

I Don't Know What "Made Love" Means

Yep, that's what my daughter wrote in her journal: "I don't know what 'made love' means."

Let me explain.

In the last couple of years, the process of developing what eventually became *But-Kickers: Growing Your Faith Bigger than Your "But!"* was a big deal in our home. I was on the lookout for "big *but* faith," seeking to annihilate it wherever it lurked. And I was the super-vigilant Wonder Mom who made sure her own child didn't fall into that shallow belief pit that refuses to acknowledge the blessing of a cloudy day or a stubbed toe.

So how did I do it?

With the Word of God, of course. I figured, *Hey, I'll have Kaki read through the whole Bible just like I'm reading through the whole Bible, and we'll talk over those faith issues that make you say, "Huh?" I'll even have her write out her observations . . . So what if she's just five weeks out of first grade?*

Several days later, after going through a couple of chapters of Genesis together, I was thoroughly impressed with my little genius. She wondered what it meant to be cursed, whether snakes used to have legs or if they hopped around on their tails, and she wondered if any of the fish God created looked like Nemo.

Then came Genesis 4. At this point I was convinced Kaki could fly solo, so I queued up BibleGateway.com so she could hear the Word while following along in her Bible.

I walked away to give her a chance to work alone.

A few minutes later when I checked to see how she was doing, I found that she had already finished the chapter and written her observations. Great over-estimator of reality that I am, I was ready for Kaki to ask why Cain was so angry, why God liked some offerings but not others, or why a man would have two wives.

Instead, I saw Kaki with a confused look on her face as she showed me what she had written: *I don't know what "made love" means.*

She had never gotten past verse one of Genesis 4: *Adam made love to his wife, Eve . . .*

And from what she could see, virtually everything else in the chapter hinged on at least a casual understanding of what verse one meant.

So much for the deep, theological discussion on faith-bearing issues. She had one simple question.

And so I answered it with a bird, a bee, and a boatload of hugs and kisses.

Then we were done.

At least for that day.

I'm so thankful for God who fathers me in much the same way—often using people He has strategically placed in my life to be His mouthpiece and His arms.

When I suffered heartbreak as a new Christian, I begged God for a miracle, for a change in what looked like my fate without the man I thought was my soulmate.

As I searched the Scriptures looking for some hidden hermeneutic that would explain my current level of woulda-coulda-shoulda, the verse that seemed to scream at me was Matthew 16:23. Peter wanted to keep Jesus from moving closer to the cross, but Jesus responded to him: *Get behind me, Satan! You are a stumbling block to me; you do not have in mind the concerns of God, but merely human concerns.*

I stopped in my steps right there, just like Kaki did at *Adam made love to his wife, Eve.* I literally froze with my mouth hanging open. *Was God calling ME "Satan," too?* And also like my daughter, I knew that my comprehension of anything said after that would be colored by my grasp, or lack thereof, of Matthew 16: 23. Shocked and still, I waited until Carmen, my mentor and spiritual mom, in whose house I sat, came alongside me.

She practically whispered as she explained the passage saying, God had plans that were vastly different from the plans I had.

So much for the deep, theological discussion on faith-bearing issues. I had one simple question. And Carmen answered it with hot tea, tissues, and hugs.

Then we were done.

At least for that day.

I gave you milk, not solid food, for you were not yet ready for it.
~ I Corinthians 3:2

What Do You Know About God that He's Never Actually Said in His Word?

In our first six months of marriage, my husband never actually told me, but I realized he hated it when I spent an inordinate amount of time and energy preparing our home for guests. The result of my high adrenaline efforts was that I was usually too exhausted to enjoy their visit. And that was typically enough to make my husband throw up his hands, talk to himself, and then respond.

So he decided to fix me.

He opted to wait until we were packed and well on our way to Santiago, Chile, to tell me that someone would be staying in our apartment for the entire two weeks we would be gone.

Hmmm . . . He's changed a lot since then, but occasionally he slips into that haze that makes him assume other people's level of comfort with squeaky toys and Cheerios on the sofa is the same as ours. Living with him and sharing life have made me aware of this tidbit of his character profile and have made me a little less likely to serve up a piece of my mind for dinner at night.

It's all about relationship.

Living and walking with Christ has likewise opened my eyes to aspects of *His* character that I would not have known otherwise. I know for instance that He, God Almighty, likes to wink at me.

Yes, *wink* at me.

And only He would have known that, in the secret place of my heart, I have always wanted my father to wink at me. I've always wanted to know I was that special girl for whom He would move heaven and earth.

Then years ago on a typically dark night in the Peruvian Amazon, though I couldn't see my hand in front of my face, I noticed the sky was especially clear and bright. I was amazed at the sheer beauty and expanse of what lay overhead, and I said so out loud to God.

A moment later, one of the stars suddenly shone brighter than all the rest as it shimmied its way apart from the others and back again. It was as if God Himself winked at me and said, "Oh, if you like *that*, you haven't seen anything yet!"

He knew I would see that shimmy as a wink, knew I'd be left there with my mouth hanging open, knew how tremendously it would lift my heart in that moment, knew I would immediately connect that wink to something I've longed for since childhood, and knew I would understand that part of His being my Heavenly Father would include gifting me with what my earthly father never did. He knew *me*.

It's all about relationship.

What do *you* know about God that He hasn't actually said in His Word? What is that secret that only you and He share? When did He move heaven and earth in such a way that you had no trouble recognizing His mighty hand?

How sweet are your words to my taste, sweeter than honey to my mouth!
~ Psalm 119:103

Relationships in the Wild

Recently, in a seminar I taught, we discussed "Relationships in the Wild," the best verbiage I could think of to describe the resolute craziness of events in Judges 19. The history found here recounts events in the life of a woman whose name we do not know and whose voice we do not hear.

Although this narrative is commonly referred to as "A Levite and His Concubine," flee from the notion that this simplistic title depicts the depths to which this account reaches.

Nothing New Under the Sun

In this horror story, every type of relationship dynamic is explored, all in the context of anarchy—when Israel has no king, no judge, and no recognition of God as their leader. Culture and impulse rule, and the resulting savagery is enough to lift our eyebrows, even in the twenty-first century.

When a mob of men is denied sexual favors with a new man in town, they are satiated by an all-night rape-fest with the new man's mistress who is thrown to them like meat to hungry dogs.

> The connections between men and their calling, between men and women, between men and men, between fathers-in-law and sons-in-law, between fathers and daughters, between culture and law, between power and freedom, and between right and wrong are displayed in such a way as to give us a textbook definition of barbarianism.
>
> Nobody gets it right.

Seriously?
So why is the mistress/concubine given over to satisfy the lust of these men? Because, apparently, she won the bid over the virgin daughter of the savages' neighbor, who himself offered the savages the chance to do anything they wanted with his virgin daughter if they would only leave the new man alone.

Not only does the new man, the Levite, throw his concubine out to the vicious mob to do with her as they please, but the next morning he exits the house with no apparent regard for her well-being. The Levite steps over the woman, *his* woman, *his* sex slave, who has collapsed at the doorway of the house with her arms outstretched. He shouts at her as he leaves.

"Get up; let's go," he says in Judges 19:28 as if she's been out shopping too long at the marketplace, and he's ready to go home.

And when there is no response, the Levite puts the woman on his donkey and leaves.

Read it for yourself, please!

The connections between men and their calling, between men and women, between men and men, between fathers-in-law and sons-in-law, between fathers and daughters, between culture and law, between power and freedom, and between right and wrong are displayed in such a way as to give us a textbook definition of barbarianism.

Nobody gets it right.

The Unthinkable

The first chapter of this story ends with the new man, the Levite, the owner of the concubine/second-class wife, cutting up his post-rape call girl into twelve pieces (something he may have learned in Levite training) and mailing a piece of her body to each of the twelve tribes of Israel.

He wants the men of the tribe of Benjamin to be so despised for raping his concubine that the rest of Israel would punish them.

He sees no guilt of his own.

His supposed righteousness is built on the shoulders of other men's sin.

Regardless of how many times I have read this narrative, by the end of the seminar I had to admit I was more outraged than ever before by the heinous, unbridled acts of depravity found in this story.

Done with That

I wanted to say I was over it—that by hanging out in the Book of Judges with story after story about marred relationships between every conceivable population, I had found enough mentions of God's name to be satisfied.

But that simply wasn't true.

Then I realized I wasn't supposed to feel satisfied.

God's Plan

Why? Because God's plan is to call our attention to Him, and if that doesn't happen for you as you wade through the anarchy and godlessness of Judges, I'm not sure what will.

What questions do we ask when we read of a girl whose fate is to become, like an animal, a burnt offering because of a promise made, not by her, but by her father? (Judges 11)

How do we feel when we come across a newly married woman forced to sleep with the best man from her wedding and later burned to death as recompense for her husband's reaction to it? (Judges 14 and 15)

And how do we respond when a man offers his virgin daughter to a mob of rapists to dissuade the mob from its desire to have sex with a male guest at the man's house? (Judges 19)

Or when a Levite in his devout delirium cuts up his sex slave and sends her body parts to people he hopes will be outraged by someone else's ferocious acts of viciousness against her? (Judges 20)

Help!
Should we not beg for God's enlightenment here? Should we not plead for a reason to hope even when so many in these pages are ravished to death by unthinkable sin or when the fate of the unsuspecting is marked by the deeds of the savage?

And would our great God not respond by urging us, the blood-washed righteous ones, into holy confession by prompting the lips of our hearts to utter the words, "*The savage, my kinsman,*" as Elisabeth Elliot did in her book by that name?

Elisabeth's missionary husband was speared to death in the Ecuadorian jungle by an Auca Indian whom she later led to Christ. No one even thinks to do that until she understands she is no less savage than a homicidal Auca when she walks away from God and chooses to live in darkness rather than light.

Neither are we.

The next time I take a look at the Book of Judges, I hope I see the reflection I cast when I choose what seems right in my own eyes only.

And I hope it scares me to life.

. . . Do not think of yourself more highly than you ought, but rather think of yourself with sober judgment, in accordance with the faith God has distributed to each of you.
~ Romans 12:3

The Miracle Worker

I am outraged every single time I hear someone steal God's glory by claiming that God no longer performs miracles today.

These perpetrators usually have seven letters after their name, and they usually begin their arguments with something like, "Now that the Scriptures are complete . . ."

My response to that rationale is, "Huh?"

Putting God Back into Faith

It is indeed possible to be too educated for our own good and to relegate God and His work to a box shallow enough for a tadpole to stand in. The sun does not have to stand still, nor does anyone have to trod through a sea on dry land in order for us to claim an event as "inexplicable by the laws of nature [and therefore] held to be supernatural in origin or an act of God" (TheFreeDictionary.com).

Who do these perpetrators think changes the sentiment of a disgruntled woman at her abortion appointment and causes her to fall in love with her baby? Who do they think causes a man who loses his wife and the child she clutched in a fatal shooting to understand that the deadly bullet was not random? And who do they think convinces a woman to reconcile with her adulterous husband and to mother the child born to him and his mistress?

All these are present-day miracles clearly from the hand of Almighty God. He works to convince us that His ultimate plan for each person requires the outworking of the inexplicable, of the supernatural, and of the just plain weird in our lives.

> Were it not for the depth of her pain, the melody—the miracle that sweetness comes forth from bitterness, would not have been so pleasing, nor would it have ministered to me regarding my own similar hurts.

In fact, once my sisters-in-law and I were listening to a favorite song of ours as sung by three different performers. All three singers delivered a technically perfect rendition of the song, but as we compared the three on a more subjective scale, only the first made our toes curl in our shoes. She was clearly the only one who had suffered hurt long enough and deeply enough to put an authentic spin on a dramatic song, expressing the heart and rage of a recently-jilted woman.

The second and third performers sounded as though they were singing about someone else's scars, but we just knew that first woman had been in the pit and had found that only Jesus could dig her out.

Her raw, guttural interpretation of the lyrics was so real that we vicariously experienced her pain, nearly to the point of tears. Were it not for the depth of her pain, the melody—the miracle that sweetness comes forth from bitterness, would not have been so pleasing, nor would it have ministered to me regarding my own similar hurts.

No, miracles are not dead today, and neither is the One who brings them forth.

Thanksgiving

So, in the spirit of Thanksgiving I bend my knees to the real Miracle Worker—to the One who caused me to see my beauty when man called me ugly, to turn on the light when I preferred to live in darkness, to stand before strangers and declare my abusive past, to stand before well-known ones and do the same, and to call good that which has nearly destroyed me because I knew God would ultimately use it to compose a sweet melody that would fall from my lips.

These melodies are the miracles of my life and the handprints of God all over me.

And He plays those melodies over and over and over again.

Let the redeemed of the Lord tell their story—those he redeemed from the hand of the foe.
~ Psalm 107:2

What You Should Know About the God of Resurrection

"Word!" "Testify!" "Amen and amen!" Shouts of praise ushered me back to my childhood roots as we joined hundreds of people in New York City on Easter and celebrated the Resurrection of Jesus Christ.

Hearing, Feeling and Tasting the Cross
We worshipped through a dramatic presentation of the last week of Christ's earthly life—a presentation so poignant I could almost hear the ripping of the veil in the temple, feel my chest cavity fight to keep from suffocating, and taste the blood that dripped from that thorn-crowned brow.

And as scandalous as the death of Christ was, His resurrection was that much more magnificent. The grave could not hold Him any more than a womb can hold the baby whom

God summons to the light with that last feverish push.

The God of Resurrection

But know this about the God of Resurrection, and shout it from the rooftop: You don't have to be dead and in a grave for God to lift you up. Sometimes He resurrects the living!

This God of Resurrection lifts up the distraught, slave-wife, Hagar (Genesis, chapters 16 and 21), as she cries out to Him on the run, lifts up a drunken-looking Hannah as she begs Him for a child (I Samuel 1), lifts up a perpetually bleeding woman (Luke 8) in a culture that calls moderately bleeding women unclean, and, in each case, He gives the woman courage to do what she would never ordinarily do.

Hagar returns to a difficult living situation, but with a renewed vision of herself after interacting with the God who sees her. Hannah gets the baby for whom she begged, and then she gives him back to the Lord by having him live far away from home in a temple where he can serve God all of his days. And the untouchable, bleeding woman—forbidden to enter the temple or synagogue—touches the hem of Jesus' robe to be made well. All of these women had been slaves to their relationships, their desires, or their culture. The touch of God gave them a freedom in their circumstances of which they could have only dreamt.

And you, if you know the God of Resurrection, if Jesus Christ has paid your ransom, why do you insist on slavery? He has opened your shackles with the only key that fits, and He has called you to shake off those chains.

Be free!

> You don't have to be dead and in a grave for God to lift you up. Sometimes He resurrects the living!

So if the Son sets you free, you will be free indeed.
~ John 8:36

Hope for the Cheerful: Because the Hurting Already Know What to Do

Isn't it strange that there's a huge, gaping hole in the outpouring of hope for the ones who most need it, yet who are least likely to seek it—the cheerful?

"That's Okay. I'm Good."
The happy-go-lucky, got-a-click-in-my-step and-a-dollar-in-the-bank crew is so overwhelmed with momentary goodness, they never suspect there's a reason to even think about, much less invest in, long-term bliss.

The hurting, however, know exactly what to do, because they must. And if a hurting person isn't looking for ways to pad their knees and plug their ears from excessive kneeling and screaming out to

God, I'll bet—as my grandma used to say, "They haven't hurt bad enough for long enough."

Ice Cream Goodness

Think of offering hope to the cheerful like giving the sunny day buyer of an ice cream cone a couple of extra napkins. They may be satisfied with the simple, paper funnel, wrapped around the bottom of the cone, because they are so eager to get at the creamy yumminess.

But you, the vendor, know that unless they gulp the entire thing in one fell swoop, they will need napkins because the least little distraction or delay from licking themselves into a frenzy will cause that wonderful, icy treat to melt down their cone and down their hand into an unmanageable mess.

The succulent swirl becomes a sticky fly-trap they long to rinse off and be done with.

Gitchy-Gitchy-Goo

Or perhaps think of offering hope to the cheerful like visiting a first-time mom in the hospital and slipping a little something between her flowers, balloons, and pink lollipops—something like a booklet of coupons for free afternoons off during which you will personally take care of her child.

That mom may be too busy counting the curls in her baby's eyelashes right then to even notice, but you, the seasoned veteran, know the day is coming when that same mom would sell her ovaries for that elusive eighth consecutive hour of sleep, or for an uninterrupted trip to the restroom.

And so it is with the cheerful. When they least expect it, change happens—and the kind of change that makes them wonder if they ever should have been blessed with a child to begin with. *Surely,* she thinks, *no other mom is so anxious for a bit of respite that she goes to church just for the free babysitting.*

But you, the herald of hope, are there to tell her she is perfectly normal—that there are many moms who feel like she does—that change isn't something that happened to *her,* but something that happens, period. And you're there to tell her there's nothing wrong with longing for a moment you can call your own or wanting to read books with words in them.

Give the Word

So next time you see a friend caught up in the wiles of a triple-decker, or a mom who won't put her nineteen-month-old down long enough for her to learn to walk, offer a couple of napkins, or offer hope—not because you wish them harm, but because you wish them joy. Give them the Word—the Truth, the only lasting goodness that will have them licking their chops long after the cone is gone.

The grass withers, the flower fades, but the word of our God will stand forever.
~ Isaiah 40:8

On Wives and Handcuffs: How to Break Out of Relationship Jail

Did you know that the Spanish word for "wives," *esposas,* is the same as the Spanish word for "handcuffs"?

And, coincidentally, the similarities between wives and handcuffs go far beyond word origin and translation. They also rise above that old, insulting, ball and chain analogy, used for years by pubescent-minded men who woke up one day to find that being married meant more than showing off their virility or counting their chest hairs.

A simple comparison of wives and handcuffs can actually help anyone in the dog house break out of relationship jail and grovel his way back into the good graces of their long lost loves. So if a trip upriver for some asinine thing you've done is causing you to long for landlocked heaven, here are two easy ways to reclaim your place among puckered-up people who have someplace to go tonight:

Resist Pulling Away When You Feel Stuck

Both wives and handcuffs cause pain if you try to jerk and pull yourself away from them.

If you feel stuck, it's because you are—that is, truly bound together for life. That includes long walks across black sand beaches on Maui or shorter strolls hopping over broken Pepsi bottles at Brighton Beach in Brooklyn. Remember, even if your union ends in divorce, the remnants of your marriage will be part of who you are forever.

If you feel stuck, it's because you are—that is, truly bound together for life.

So don't be an Adam by throwing your Eve under the bus, thereby declaring yourself better off alone. Or even worse, declaring yourself better off with someone else. What real man just stands there silently when things go awry and then blames his woman for his own shortcomings? Come on!

You don't necessarily have to *do* anything at this point. It's resisting the urge to do something stupid—like pulling away or causing her to pull away—that's in play here.

And in not pulling away when you most feel stuck, you exude the greatest aphrodisiac of all—the power of *being there.*

When You Need Adjustments, Always Use the Right Key

Both wives and handcuffs open up right away when you use the right key.

Maybe you walked into your relationship with your eyes wide open. You knew you'd be handcuffed to someone else and that you wouldn't be able to avoid living in their context, in their world. You knew who you were, and you were ready to play your role opposite someone else.

Then the unthinkable happened.

Life changed.

Illness? Job commitments? A special-needs child? A normal child? Who knows? But what previously worked in your relationship doesn't work anymore. What do you do? Try to force your old way of doing things to fit your new circumstances?

That would be like trying to stuff a 42/Long into a 34/Medium and calling it good. Why walk around in child-size handcuffs if you're an adult? They'll pinch and squeeze you until there's no circulation left in your wrists and hands.

If the adjustments you do make are one-sided or prehistoric, you'll find yourself in the same position as that guy who's trying to pull his way out of a relationship altogether. But if you take a minute—a literal sixty seconds to ask your love what new look for your relationship would work best, you'll diffuse a firecracker before it's even lit.

And, in the process, you will have found another great aphrodisiac: the power of mutual submission—the agreement that God indeed will work in your life for your good and His glory through someone else.

Now go ahead. Attempt a jailbreak.

Husbands, in the same way be considerate as you live with your wives, and treat them with respect as the weaker partner and as heirs with you of the gracious gift of life, so that nothing will hinder your prayers.
~ I Peter 3:7

A Not-So-Silent Scream: What I Wish Jephthah's Daughter Had Said

The mysterious story of Jephthah's daughter makes me crazy.

Jephthah, a Jewish warrior, once rejected by his brothers and denied an inheritance for being the illegitimate son of a prostitute, has a chance to become a big shot among the Israelites if he can lead them to victory in a battle against their enemies, the Ammonites.

Jephthah's Vow

Perhaps in Jephthah's zeal to be accepted, he promises God to offer as a burnt sacrifice the first thing or person who greets him at home after the battle if God gives him that victory. God gives the victory, and Jephthah returns home to see his daughter—his only child, lead the traditional celebratory processional in honor of her father.

The destiny of Jephthah's daughter is thereby sealed.

Is This Fair to Jephthah's Daughter?

One of two things will happen to her: She will be burned to death as a sacrifice, or she will remain unmarried and childless—two fates not nearly as far apart in her culture as they may seem.

Either way, this rash vow her father makes, though completely outside the daughter's control, ensures the end of any dreams she may have for her own future. As a result, Jewish women begin a tradition of mourning this woman for four days each year.

How am I to understand the heart of a young girl who charges her father saying, "Do to me what you have promised you would do" (Judges 11:36) when the stakes are so high?

I can't.

And what's more, her only request is to have two months away with her friends in order to mourn the fact that she will never marry.

Justice

My human, justice-oriented side compels me to give Jephthah's daughter a voice that satisfies my fury for her fate and for that of many women whose harrowing stories are told in the book of Judges, a book that chronicles a time when anarchy ruled because Israel had no king.

I do not share that sympathy, however, for Jephthah, despite his rejection for something beyond *his* control and despite what probably amounted to a boyish attempt to regain a place at the dinner table that should have been his initially. I do not share that sympathy because I see myself more like Jephthah's daughter—with a life reshaped by someone without my consent.

I do not share that sympathy because I see myself more like Jephthah's daughter—with a life reshaped by someone without my consent.

The unquenched fire I carry from my abuse issues spreads into Jephthah's daughter's story, and I am pressed to extinguish it—to create my own scenario in which this young girl expresses her rage, tells it like it is, and causes Jephthah to agonize in guilt and grief.

Wouldn't This Scenario Be Better?

I wish she had written a poignant letter to her friends that eventually ended up in her father's ashen hands, and I wish that letter had given a voice to her previously silent scream.

I wish it had gone something like this:

Dear Daughters of Israel,

It is day forty-nine.

There are yet seven sunsets before I meet my Maker.

O how my heart cries within me, for this should not be my portion. How I long to join you in endless celebrations of victory with timbrels and dances, praising God for His deliverance from such as the Ammonites!

But instead, I have now become the burnt offering of my father, Jephthah. I have become his surety of peace with his Maker. For were it not for his unbreakable vow, I would be as you, O daughters of Israel—I would be as you, marrying and bearing children to be nursed at my breast. I would be as you, living long life and being laid to rest next to the husband of my youth.

But I am not like you. I am like a fugitive hiding in the mountains of Mizpeh, hoping, praying, pleading that the LORD would be my El Roi—that He would hear me as He heard Hagar—that He might deliver me as He delivered her.

Remember me, O daughters of Israel. Remember me and mourn me. Remember me, that daughter of Gilead who cried, "O God of my youth, could you not spare me this tragic end? Could you not allow me to know a man, to hold and to be held, to love and to suffer through long life—for that is my portion, is it not?"

Signed,

A Daughter of Gilead

In my scenario, this scroll letter would be hidden among the few possessions of Jephthah's daughter.

Jephthah would know nothing of it until his vow is complete.

An altar would be built. A fire lit. A daughter offered.

And once again, Jephthah would tear his clothes in despair, crying, "O that I never made such a vow, my Lord! Were it my body bound to the altar, for my daughter did nothing to deserve this. I shall never escape this torment of my soul!"

The smell of burning flesh would hang in the air and assault his senses. Two servants would build a stone memorial as Jephthah walks away.

At sundown following the Sabbath, the men would unpack the caravan which contains a pair of worn-out leather sandals, a woman's head covering, and a small scroll. They would be delivered to Jephthah immediately.

Then Jephthah would clutch the head covering in one hand and press its thick, embroidered edge against his cheek. Slowly, he would unroll the small scroll and begin to read.

I'm Still Not Satisfied. Are You?

Scenario done.

Mission accomplished.

Jephthah has been duly whipped and silenced, and my mania tranquilized, right?

Yet it is not.

And that's because, with honest introspection, I know my inability or unwillingness to have any sympathy at all, for Jephthah wars against God's purpose in giving us Jephthah's backstory in the first place.

I see the circumstances of his birth, and I refuse to care. I hear the ridicule of his half-brothers, and it makes no difference. I feel the rejection of his cohorts, and I harden my heart.

All this because of what Jephthah eventually does. Overlooking or minimizing his rash vow and its ultimate cost would be a betrayal of Jephthah's daughter with whom I identify—and, therefore, a betrayal of me.

Why I Want To See Blood

I will not join the multitudes who read this story and forget about this young girl whose name is never revealed. I will not reduce her tragic end to just another unusual circumstance of her culture. I will not let Jephthah's backstory outweigh his daughter's present story and make it of no effect.

I will, however, squeeze my grip around Jephthah's throat for being one who selfishly rewrote the script of his daughter's life without her consent because, in doing so, I vicariously avenge the tattered, stained script of my own life. I rehearse my own created scenario of how her story *should* have unfolded, and I relish the stolen satisfaction of it.

Then something happens.

I realize that is not how God wrote the story.

On Jephthah and Christ

And when I squeeze Jephthah's throat, I walk away with the blood-stained hands of one who refuses to be reconciled to God on God's terms, who refuses to see there may be more to any story God gives us in his Word than what first meets the eye, who refuses to see that Jephthah's backstory *is* indeed important because it is just like Christ's backstory concerning the circumstances of *His* birth, the ridicule of *His* half-brothers, and the rejection of *His* cohorts.

I understand the quandary, yet I strengthen my grip because I cannot be wrong. Far too much time has been invested in the "how it should have gone" side of this story for me to go back and change it now. So I rehearse my created scenario, and the stain is embedded deeper.

> Jephthah's backstory *is* indeed important because it is just like Christ's backstory concerning the circumstances of *His* birth, the ridicule of *His* half-brothers, and the rejection of *His* cohorts.

Blood-Stained Hands

The dilemma is that I don't want blood-stained hands or a struggle with the God of the universe. I don't want to be guilty of anything; I want to be in the right. With sweat and tears I soak and scrub those blood stains until my hands are fragile and raw, yet the stains remain. I rub and scrub again but to no avail.

The "Out, damn'd spot! Out, I say!" of Shakespeare's Lady Macbeth* is my echo as I realize there is no cohabitation of my rightness and my blood-stained hands. Just as she, even in her sleep, laments her role in her husband's killing of the King of Scotland and sees her own hands as stained by his blood, I, likewise, see my guilt in crucifying the King of Kings and want nothing more than to be rid of it.

Pain, Rage, and Terror—to Redemption
And so I relinquish my grip and yield to the Lord's cleansing, yield to His prerogative to create scenarios that are right in His eyes, scenarios that draw attention to sin, to Christ, to the cross, and to the needs of every man, woman, and child, scenarios that avenge those who are injured, that welcome to a better place those we think are leaving this life much sooner than they should, scenarios that soothe my pain, my rage, and my terror.

And then I take my stance under the umbrella labeled, "Those who need forgiveness"—right next to Jephthah.

Do not gloat when your enemy falls; when they stumble, do not let your heart rejoice, or the Lord will see and disapprove and turn his wrath away from them.
~ Proverbs 24:17, 18

**Macbeth, Act 5, Scene 1, Lines 26-40.*

What Happens When Survivors of Sexual Abuse Are Validated

Like me, you've probably already asked the obvious question: Why does God allow sexual abuse to begin with?

How can He, who is present everywhere, He who knows what will happen before it is ever conceived in the mind of the perpetrator, He who can easily prevent it, ever permit anyone—especially a child, to suffer a violation and humiliation that robs her of her childhood, her value, and her peace, to blame and hate herself for what is not her fault, to cringe whenever someone uses the word "purity," to be chased by her memories every time she hears *that* name, smells *that* odor, sees *that* room, or tastes *that* food, to believe that even her screams will never be heard or taken seriously, to watch others treat her perpetrator as one having done no harm, or to see his face when her husband makes should be welcome advances to her, to be convinced that no good man will ever want her, to prefer the safety of obesity to the fear of looking good, to feel like trash and to know she will never, ever be able to scrub away her filth because it comes from within?

And how can He, after allowing the unthinkable, ever expect to be called Heavenly Father or to be sought as "a refuge and strength, an ever-present help in trouble" (Psalms 46:1)?

I've wondered those very same things.

Where Was God?

It's hard enough to think of God tolerating the depravity of sexual abuse, but it's an entirely different thing to imagine Him standing in the doorway observing it—watching, as if sanctioning the casting of His own into a veritable fire. For much less, an earthly father might be jailed.

But then there's Daniel, chapter three.

This story of three exploited Hebrew men changes everything.

When the three men refuse to dishonor their God by worshipping a golden image, soldiers report them to the King of Babylon. The king therefore condemns the three Hebrews to death by fire in a furnace seven times hotter than normal. The fierce heat engulfs and destroys the soldiers who carry Shadrach, Meshach, and Abednego, with hands and feet bound, to their supposed death. Yet once they are in the furnace, the king sees the three Hebrews walking around unbound and unhurt. And with them in the fire he sees a fourth man walking around, also unbound and unhurt, "who looks like a son of the gods." The king orders them out of the furnace and notices they are unscathed, and that they don't even smell like smoke!

Why? Because God didn't intend for them to bear the scars of fire, nor did He intend for passersby to be triggered to the memory of flames at the smell of smoke on them.

Like abuse victims, these men are cast into that furnace without their permission and for no fault of their own.

Why Devastation Is Necessary

Yet the blaze is necessary. If you never walk through fire, you'll never believe God is present in it, that He has a solution for overwhelming flames, or that He wants to be known on a deeper level than you already know Him—as the God who walks with you through the inferno.

And once He delivers you from that fire, He wants you, everyone watching you, and everyone, everywhere who even hears about you to know there is nothing too heinous for Him to heal, and that He, God, is powerful not only to free you from the devastating destruction of fire, but also to place you in a position of wellbeing and favor—not by extinguishing the fire, but by walking with you while the flames still burn.

Validation of Your Pain

And though He delivers you whole, He does not consider it a small thing for you to have endured the process. The greatest validation of your pain and mine is the fact that the outer heat of that furnace is indeed deadly—so much so that it engulfs and eliminates strong soldiers who are overcome by the heat emanating from the fire without ever having been immersed in it.

Even amid fitful cries and screams, even while gritting her teeth and declaring what she might later regret, the woman of faith has to allow the Word of God to validate her and to change her, or else she has no hope.

Even amid fitful cries and screams, even while gritting her teeth and declaring what she might later regret, the woman of faith has to allow the Word of God to validate her and to change her, or else she has no hope.

And when people see you are all right despite the horrific story of your life—that you have a sense of victory they can't explain, they know that God has somehow intervened because there is no other explanation that fits.

That's when it becomes clear to you, everyone watching you, and everyone, everywhere who even hears about you that your faith is not a cheap faith that can rejoice but cannot weep—or that is victorious only when you are shielded from atrocities like rape, abuse, and assault, when you are spared all the emotional upheaval of recurring nightmares, or when, in this life, you are rewarded for all your good works. That type of life requires nothing more than the faith alleged by a good fortune cookie. It does not require the blood of Christ.

For those Hebrew men God exchanges the scars of fire for the wholeness of deliverance, and He can do the same for you. Remember that the same king who orders them to the furnace later causes them to prosper by promoting them in the province of Babylon. And in later years their voices and their story are indeed heard.

"... They saw that the fire had not harmed their bodies, nor was a hair of their heads singed; their robes were not scorched, and there was no smell of fire on them."
~ Daniel 3:27

Acknowledgments

For all you who wonder about such things, like writing a book, it takes much more than a village; it takes prayer.

And *but*-kicking.

So thank you, from the depths of my plus-size soul, to all who have walked this road with me in one way or another. *I thank my God upon every remembrance of you.* (Philippians 1:3 KJV)

I think especially of:

Barbara Morgan, a great lady and my precious mom, whose staggering life story makes her the biggest But-Kicker any of us will ever know.

All my *sistahs,* gifted to me by the good Lord who knew I needed them.

Sharon-Ann Sealey-Fletcher, who has uplifted me since fourth grade.

The fabulous Warrior Writing Women of Clarks Summit: Leslee Clapp, Barbara Engle, Rebecca Loescher, Gail Mills, Cindy Noonan, Sarah Lynn Phillips and Jo Ann Walczak, who make the art of writing a fun and necessary adventure.

Diana Flegal of Hartline Literary Agency, who is as much a literary agent as she is a trusted friend and prayer partner.

Vonda Skelton, Carolyn Knefely, and the inspiring women of Christian Communicators, who help me remember that there is eternal purpose in what we do for Christ.

Yvonne Ortega, author of *Finding Hope for Your Journey through Breast Cancer* and *From Broken to Beautiful,* whose inspiring journey makes me try harder—over and over again.

Kim Gromacki and the women of the best Wednesday night Ladies' Bible Study around, who have prayed not only through the publishing of this book, but also through many of the events described in its pages.

Peggy Walker, my hilarious mentor, who has no idea how often she has lit a fire without ever striking a match.

Julie Manwarren, my "iron-sharpening-iron" friend.

Carol King, Joseph Cartuccio, Larry Ramsey, and Sadie Herman, who get more from their students because they expect more.

Kristi Parker, whose expertise in layout is exceeded only by her ability to answer the question, "Huh?" without laughing even once.

And Jo Ann Walczak, my editor and friend, whose attention to detail makes me hope I never see her when I have chocolate in my teeth.

May God be known in every place. He has done great things!